The Jesus Question

Daring to Walk the Path of Peace

The Jesus Question

Daring to Walk the Path of Peace

Christie Monson

To the children of every country:
May you grow and thrive
in a peace-loving world

Contents

Preface

Standing in my Minnesota garden, I scanned the sky that was uncharacteristically quiet due to the temporary ban on flying. On September 11, 2001, the epicenter of the chaos and terror was on our east coast. But we all felt vulnerable. After the initial shock, many people said, "Now we know what it feels like for people of other countries who have been attacked throughout history." (It had been sixty years since Pearl Harbor—a lifetime for many.) Then waves of fear, anger, and thirst for retaliation began to show themselves in the news and online. In spite of the seriousness of the attack on us, in spite of understanding the fear that people felt, something didn't fit for me.

It reminded me of my childhood in Berkeley, California. Through most of the sixties and the early seventies, we lived alongside the raging protests against the Vietnam War. As a child viewing the damage caused by the violence, I wondered, "How can people show they want peace by acting violently?" This never made sense to me.

And now my country was going to attack another. Not the architects of the attack on us, but someone else. My simple logic returned to me: why were we creating more violence when we know now, more than ever, what it feels like?

As a teacher, I began to hear children talk about war with excitement. Some expressed a desire to go to war and shoot people. I found this alarming, not only that they saw this as a way to become a hero, but that many of the adults around them were not alarmed to hear of these ambitions.

My next questions came from the fact that even though our constitution purports freedom to practice any religion, many people say that ours is a Christian nation. When hearing the cries for war, I began to ask, where is the Christian ethic of forgiveness? In this country that I love, where is our motivation to take the high road? We have many politicians who win votes by saying that they are Christian. To be a Christian means to follow Jesus, to live according to the life and teachings of Jesus. But we all know that throughout history, people who call themselves Christians have demonstrated both constructive and destructive behavior. So we must be vigilant and ask ourselves if we are honestly following Jesus's example in any given situation.

When our nation attacked Iraq, I felt that we were making a disastrous choice. It gnawed at me that our leaders were touting their Christian identity more than ever, when killing unarmed civilians, torturing our fellow human beings, and refusing prisoners a trial are actions that Jesus would never advocate.

As these atrocities continued, I agonized over the path that our nation was taking. I wrote an essay addressing these issues. I sent it to every Christian I knew. I hoped that, rather than supporting leaders according to lip service or party affiliation, Christians would follow a path more in alignment with peacemaking, since this is the example that Jesus set for us.

Many people told me how valuable the essay was to them. Still, our country continued to move forward with the violence, using cries of fear to keep the support going. I continued to dialogue with conservative and liberal Christians, with Jews, Muslims, and Buddhists in my community, as well as those with no religious affiliation. I continued to write letters to my representatives and letters to the editor. None of this felt effective. Friends encouraged me to publish my essay. Many felt that I should expand it into a book and include more details about how following Jesus applies to specific world events.

I felt certain this is what I needed to do. It concerned me that Jesus has often been shoved aside in many decisions that Christians face. Not only did I feel an urgent need to examine our actions in the current international crisis, but this examination is needed in every part of our lives. We need to make decisions with our eyes wide open to what we believe and how we want our values to be manifested in the world.

While following a path of peace, I have never lost sight of the risk we take by doing so. Yet because of my own experiences while following Jesus, I cannot hesitate to move forward in this way.

While this book comes as a response to our country's choice to be at war, it also comes from a lifetime of learning about Jesus and what it means to follow him. I became familiar with the Bible from a very young age. I read it thoroughly with Sunday school teachers, my youth group, my family, and on my own. I loved learning about how Moses wandered the wilderness and followed God's lead even though he often felt unsure, how Jacob wrestled with God, how Samuel was open and willing to listen to God from a very young age, how Jesus brought a message of love and compassion in the most trying of times.

I was also fortunate to grow up in a church that encouraged discussions of difficult topics. Being located next to the UC Berkeley campus, we had frequent dialogues with students and street people, all of varying backgrounds. We had intergenerational discussions. We got involved in what was happening in our community and our world. I did my own wrestling with God. These dialogues and observations led me to examine how we traditionally behave in a "Christian" society, and ask whether or not that is consistent with what Jesus said and did. I continued studying these issues as an adult in churches in Tacoma, Washington, and St. Paul, Minnesota.

Understandably, after the attacks of September 11, people were afraid. It is natural to get caught up in our concerns for our safety and security. It is wise to discuss strategy after such a shattering event. We can easily be tempted to support a path of violence and military might. But the human race has followed this course throughout the centuries; can our world become less violent by bringing more violence into it? Or should we try a new strategy and take Jesus more seriously?

If we intend to follow Jesus, we must re-examine our core beliefs. We must return to his words and actions. We must follow his example to find the fullest expression of what it means to be Christian.

Do we know how such choices will turn out? No. But what does it say about our faith if we only follow Jesus when life is running smoothly for us?

It is my hope in writing this that we will remember the compassion we have been given and were meant to share.

One of the teachers of the law came and heard them debating. Noticing that Jesus had given them a good answer, he asked him, "Of all the commandments, which is the most important?"

"The most important one," answered Jesus, "is this: 'Hear O Israel, the Lord our God, the Lord is one. Love the Lord your God with all your heart and with all your soul and with all your mind and with all your strength.' The second is this: 'Love your neighbor as yourself.' There is no commandment greater than these." (Mark 12:28–31, NIV)

⧈ Standing on the Edge

The little boy hoisted himself, tummy first, onto the chair. He stood, turned to face the screen, and grabbed the controls. The game started automatically. From his point of view, the little boy played the part of a man running down an alley, automatic weapon in hand, chasing another man. Whenever his prey came into view, he worked the controls and shot to kill. The speed of the chase increased, with the man's voice of the role he played urging him on. Now the child was on the edge of the chair, which threatened to topple its support from him as he jerked and shifted his little body to complete his mission.

I was in a big-box store, in an aisle near the game department. I watched this little boy, whose size and motor coordination told me that he was probably about three years old. As horrified as I felt about a little child being exposed to adrenaline-producing scenarios and encouraged to kill, I was more shocked that his mother, standing a few feet behind him, had told him that it was all right to go play this game, and then watched and listened to the entire scene with a completely nonchalant expression. It appeared that she was not surprised or concerned about what her child was being trained to do.

I felt pulled to say something to her. But what could I say? I racked my brain, but found that most of my response came from my anxious stomach. Would a confrontation, especially one that criticized a parent's judgment, ever be an effective approach? I doubted that the woman would have blinked her eyes, as if awakening, and said, "Oh my gosh, you're right! This is not appropriate for my little boy! I want him to be a peacemaker in the world! Thank you so much for bringing this to my attention!" I was certain that even if I could find gentle words, they might have led to an altercation. Was this woman likely to react in anger or violence? Or would she be passive, not seeing what the problem was? And who was I to attempt to enlighten her? I imagined her yelling at me. I left the store.

Inside my car, I couldn't start the engine to drive away. Nor would my limbs move to get out of the car. I held onto the steering wheel and practiced in my mind what I could have said to the mother. I considered talking to a manager or writing a letter to the corporation. While stores no longer provide chairs for the comfort of their customers, I questioned the conspicuous placement of a chair next to this video game display unit so that a small child could reach it. I struggled to get a breath, distressed from thinking that someone could sell these realistic animations of hunting to kill other human beings in the first place. I wanted to do something constructive for all of us. But I'm a chicken when it comes to getting yelled at.

This scene occurred shortly after September 11, 2001. Violent video games had been around long before this, but some of my hesitation to approach the mother came from knowing that many people in our country were freshly motivated to go to war to protect our country from terrorism. As much as I could sympathize with the pain and fear people were feeling, the thought of training three-year-olds to become familiar with images of chasing and killing another human being was toxic and churned inside me. I agonized over the fervor for conflict that can overtake a society. I grieved that transforming violent scenarios into entertainment takes us even further from the goodness that God declared was in us when we were created. Where could healing begin? How could we find hope? Who would guide us?

What Would Jesus Do?

While thinking about the difficult questions we often face, I spoke with a second-grade boy who was wearing a bracelet with the initials "WWJD." He explained, "These letters stand for 'What would Jesus do?' We learn in church that wherever we are, no matter what choice we need to make, we should ask ourselves that question. This helps us to make the right decision."

By asking what Jesus would do in our own situations, we define ourselves as Christians. In most dictionaries, a *Christian* is described as one who lives according to the life and teachings of Jesus and imitates his attitudes and behaviors as closely as possible in one's daily life. In many circles, being Christian has also been associated with showing a loving concern or humane spirit toward others. For instance, one might say, "He is a good Christian" when someone has done a good deed. On the other hand, some people have suffered prejudice or violence at the hands of people who call themselves Christians, in which case, being Christian would be associated with being narrow-minded or cruel. There is clearly a need to end such confusion. If being Christian means that we imitate Jesus, we must make ourselves more consistently aware of the example that his life gave us.

When we strive to imitate Jesus, it is natural to wonder what he would do in circumstances similar to our current predicaments, especially when violence is an issue. I wonder how Jesus would have responded to the mother in the store. He rarely walked right up to someone, uninvited, and told them to get their act together. Instead, most of our Gospel accounts show that *people came to him* to learn and to be healed. He ministered to those who asked. While he didn't push himself on others, his identity and ministry were publicly known. Word spread of healings and other miracles. People were drawn to him. They knew he had something meaningful to offer.

How does this apply to us? We might not be able to perform the miracles that he did, but we can show love. We can choose nonviolence. We can participate in forming public policies that promote his ministry of compassion. Because this is sometimes met with resistance, we need to be certain of who we are and what we stand for. Jesus told us to love our enemies, but many people urge us to do otherwise. Before we take action, it is imperative that we ask ourselves the question, are we Christians in name only, or do we genuinely follow Jesus and his teachings?

We have many examples of how Jesus dealt with those who opposed him. Consider the choices that he made in the garden of Gethsemane when Judas arrived with the chief priests and temple officials:

> Then the men stepped forward, seized Jesus, and arrested him. With that, one of Jesus' companions reached for his sword, drew it out, and struck the servant of the high priest, cutting off his ear.
>
> "Put your sword back in its place," Jesus said to him, "for all who draw the sword will die by the sword." (Matthew 26:50–52, NIV)

Another Gospel account describes the scene this way:

> When Jesus' followers saw what was going to happen, they said, "Lord, should we strike with our swords?" And one of them struck the servant of the high priest, cutting off his right ear. But Je-

sus answered, "No more of this!" And
he touched the man's ear and healed
him. (Luke 22:49–51, NIV)

If ever there were justification for using a sword,
the Gethsemane scene would have been it—to defend a holy man. But if Jesus told his followers to
put away their swords, how can we justify pulling
our swords—for any reason?

▦ We React to Pain and Fear with Anger

An injured or cornered animal fears for its life, and it will strike out at anyone coming near who might present a threat. When humans are hurt, individually or nationally, the primitive part of us wants *someone* to pay. We initially react to pain as if in an early stage of emotional development, operating on reflex rather than clear thought. Often subconscious, this fear-based behavior is attuned to our very survival. If we are not able to find the perpetrator immediately after an injustice, our base emotions may entice us to "even the score" by harming our most convenient suspect, who did not necessarily commit the injustice. We have seen this phenomenon in hate crimes committed in our own country, as well as in our current international crisis.

After September 11, 2001, Osama bin Laden acknowledged that he was behind the attack on the United States. When we were not able to track him down and bring him to justice immediately, our attention quickly moved to Iraq. While there were certainly terrible things happening under Saddam's rule, there was never any proof that he was involved in the attacks on the U.S., nor was there proof that he had weapons of mass destruction. Yet many Americans felt a fervor for action, and it was easier to attack a stationery target than to locate and capture the person who actually orchestrated the attack on us.

Between March 2003 and August 2008, U.S. troop fatalities in Iraq reached 4,150. We rarely hear any mention of the deaths of soldiers from other countries fighting in Iraq, but the United Kingdom, Italy, Poland, Ukraine, Bulgaria, Spain, Denmark, El Salvador, Georgia, Slovakia, Latvia, Romania, Australia, Estonia, Netherlands, Thailand, Azerbaijan, Czech Republic, Hungary, Kazakhstan, and South Korea together lost an additional 314 people during that period, bringing total coalition deaths to 4,464.[1]

Figures on the number of wounded vary. Amy Goodman of *Democracy Now!* reports, "Typically unmentioned alongside the count of U.S. war dead are the tens of thousands of wounded (not to mention the Iraqi dead). The Pentagon doesn't tout the number of U.S. injured, but the web site icasualties.

---

1   icasualties.org, "Iraq Coalition Casualty Count," http://www.icasualties.org/ oif/DeathsByCountry.aspx.

org reports an official number of more than 40,000 soldiers requiring medical airlifts out of Iraq, a good indicator of the scale of major injuries. That doesn't include many others. Dr. Arthur Blank, an expert on post-traumatic stress disorder (PTSD), estimates that 30 percent of Iraq veterans will suffer from PTSD."[2]

How many Iraqis have died so far? Certainly some of the people who have died chose to fight. But most were unarmed civilians. National Public Radio (NPR), in their segment "The Toll of War,"[3] presented figures from a variety of sources. Following is a table that NPR provided with varying tallies of Iraqi deaths. The counts are not easy to compare, since the time periods and methods used vary, but they give us an idea of the discrepancy between the cost to invading forces and to residents.

---

2   Amy Goodman, "Body of War," *Democracy Now! The War and Peace Report*, http://www.democracynow.org/blog/2008/3/27/amy_goodmans_new_column_body_of_war.

3   NPR, "The Toll of War," http://www.npr.org/news/specials/tollofwar/tollofwarmain.html.

Iraqi Security Force and Civilian Fatalities in Iraq Since March 2003[4]

Source	Dates	Civilian Deaths
Bush Administration	March 2003– December 2005	30,000
Iraq Body Count	January 2003– April 2008	90,782
Brookings Institution	May 2003– November 2007	97,190
World Health Organization	March 2003– June 2006	151,000
Johns Hopkins School of Public Health	March 2003– July 2006	650,000

Does any of this killing represent reasonable strategy? Even if the real culprit of a crime is attacked, the "score" never becomes even. History shows us that when we try to fight fire with fire, the result is simply more fire. For how many centuries have we humans been fighting wars? People continue creating enemies for racial, ethnic, national, financial, or religious reasons. But the deeper reason for such lashing out is our basic fear when feeling threatened.

We React to Pain and Fear with Anger

4   Comments provided by NPR about methods used to reach these figures:

Bush Administration
President Bush has refused to give any numbers for Iraqi fatalities since late 2005, when he estimated that 30,000 Iraqi civilians had been killed. The Pentagon told NPR in December 2006 that it doesn't track Iraqi civilian deaths, and that it considered the Iraq Health Ministry to be the best source for a death count.

Iraqi Body Count
An independent organization run by peace activists, IBC bases its number of civilian deaths on international news reports. IBC tallies all civilian deaths attributed to military intervention in Iraq, including crimes from the breakdown of law and order. Two independent media sources must corroborate every incident before the IBC cites it. IBC is likely to underestimate violent deaths because a substantial number do not appear in media sources.

Brookings Institution
Brookings initially tried to estimate only civilians killed by "acts of war," tracking crime separately. But in January 2006, the think tank decided it was impossible to tell which deaths were caused by crime versus war. It now uses U.N. data, which tracks all violent deaths through bodies brought to hospitals and morgues. The U.N. says 34,452 civilians were killed and 36,685 were wounded in Iraq in 2006 alone. For 2007, Brookings uses data from congressional testimony by Gen. David Petraeus and the U.S. Department of Defense.

World Health Organization
A World Health Organization and Iraq Ministry of Health survey of 9,345 households in nearly 1,000 neighborhoods across Iraq estimates that 151,000 Iraqis died in violence by June 2006. Family members were asked to report deaths, and those responses were used to estimate Iraq's overall death toll since the U.S. invasion. More than half of the violent deaths occurred in Baghdad. An earlier, widely reported household survey by Johns Hopkins gave a much higher number. But the WHO survey is larger, and thus considered more accurate.

Johns Hopkins School of Public Health
Iraqi medical researchers visited 2,000 homes across the country, asking about births and deaths since January 2002. After calculating a pre- and post-invasion death rate, researchers estimated 650,000 deaths, civilian and military, as a "consequence of war." That number isn't an exact figure; statistical uncertainty means the number of Iraqi deaths could range from 400,000 to 900,000. The study is considered sound but controversial because it far outpaces other estimates.

Don't Be Afraid

Many who claim to be Christian do not hesitate to lie, kill God's children, and teach others to do the same. If someone feels that their way of life is threatened, they may use recurring cries of fear to encourage support for violence. When Christians respond in this way, they are misrepresenting Jesus. Is this our best response to the Son of God, who went to the trouble of coming here to minister to us, love us, and teach us about the Kingdom of God? What does our scripture say about basing our motivations on fear?

> There is no fear in love, but perfect love casts out fear; for fear has to do with punishment, and whoever fears has not reached perfection in love. (1 John 4:18, NRSV)

Throughout the Old and New Testaments, God, prophets, angels, and Jesus tell us not to be afraid.

In the Gospels alone, we are told thirty-four times not to be afraid or not to worry. It is worth noting that, more often than not, what shortly follows these words is one of the following: assurance that God will bring us through difficult times, a reminder of the great things God has done or will do, or a promise of the presence of Jesus or the Holy Spirit. Here are some examples:

- An angel tells Mary not to be afraid. She has found favor with God and she is pregnant with Jesus. (Luke 1:30, Matthew 1:20, Luke 1:13)

- An angel tells the shepherds, "Do not be afraid. I bring you good news of great joy that will be for all the people." [Jesus is born.] (Luke 2:10, NIV)

- Jesus tells his disciples not to be afraid of people who harass them for following him. He tells them that they will be given what to say by the Holy Spirit. He tells them not to be afraid of those who may kill the body but cannot kill the soul. (Matthew 10:26 and 28, Luke 12:4)

- Jesus says that indeed "the very hairs of your head are all numbered. Don't be afraid; you are worth more than many sparrows." (Luke 12:7, NIV; see also Matthew 10:31)

- Jesus, after talking about not needing to worry, says, "Do not be afraid, little flock, for your Father [God] has been pleased to give you the kingdom." (Luke 12:32, NIV)

- When the daughter of the synagogue ruler died, Jesus said to him, "Don't be afraid; just believe and she will be healed," and she got up. (Luke 8:50, NIV; see also Mark 5:36)

- Jesus, walking on the water toward the disciples, said, "Take courage! It is I. Don't be afraid." (Matthew 14:27, NIV; see also Mark 6:51, John 6:20; Luke 5:11)

- An angel says to the women at the tomb, "Do not be afraid, for I know that you are looking for Jesus, who was crucified. He is not here; he has risen, just as he said." (Matthew 28:5–6, NIV; see also Matthew 28:10)

- Jesus says, "Peace I leave with you; my peace I give you. I do not give to you as the world gives. Do not let your hearts be troubled and do not be afraid." (John 14:27, NIV)

Because Jesus exhorts us to live peacefully and without fear, we know that violent choices are unlike his goals for us. When we follow him, he reassures us that we need not fear doing so. In the following example, when he faced rejection and it was suggested that he could retaliate, he chose to prevent conflict.

> And he sent messengers on ahead, who went into a Samaritan village to get things ready for him, but the people there did not welcome him, because he was heading for Jerusalem. When the disciples James and John saw this, they asked, "Lord, do you want us to call fire down from heaven to destroy them?" But Jesus turned and rebuked them, and they went to another village. (Luke 9:52–56, NIV)

When we encounter rejection or conflict, we may feel afraid or powerless. It is natural to fear for our survival and be possessive of our freedom. But fear of loss can cause us to blame other people, political parties, religions, or nations for our problems. If we let fear guide us, we might react impulsively. We might choose a retaliatory response to the most convenient target before thinking things through. If we wish to create a more peaceful climate on earth, we must be willing to look at different sides of an issue, and we must take the time to remind ourselves of who or what determines our values before we act.

As I continue my walk with God, I see that we must actively build alternatives to violence and help to advance the prospects of peace. What are the consequences of a world steeped in combat? Too many innocent people are harmed, and those on the offense are emotionally and psychologically damaged. *Of course* I am devastated when anyone is attacked. *Of course* I think there are despots who must be stopped. But there are other ways. What does Jesus tell us to do?

> But I tell you who hear me: Love your enemies, do good to those who hate you, bless those who curse you, pray for those who mistreat you. (Luke 6:27–28, NIV)

As conscientious Christians, can we justify remaining silent while others who profess to be Christians behave in a warlike manner? There is a desperate need to call ourselves back to reason. If we allow killing in the name of "Christian America," we are as guilty as those who attack us. Who are we imitating then? We, as Christians, need to step forward and show that we are following Jesus, who tells us not to be afraid, but rather to coexist peacefully with others. This includes showing kindness and fairness. Fairness is honestly treating all parties equally, giving no more favor or advantage to one side than another. Isn't it reasonable to expect our leaders to work for this? If we hold certain standards for other countries, we must embrace the same standards for ourselves. This applies to laws as well as weapons. To say that we can do and have whatever we like, but someone else is not allowed the same privileges, is immature and unfair, and it reflects a fearful mindset. This is certainly not imitating Jesus. Rather, it reflects the mindset of bullies.

> How can you say to your brother, "Brother, let me take the speck out of your eye," when you yourself fail to see the plank in your own eye? You hypocrite, first take the plank out of your eye, and then you will see clearly to remove the speck from your brother's eye. (Luke 6:42, NIV)

Love One Another

Just as bullies initiate unprovoked attacks, especially on people smaller or weaker than themselves, I believe that initiating an unprovoked war is an act of bullying on a large scale—otherwise known as terrorism. How can a rational adult agree with such tactics? What do we hope to teach our children by this? What does Jesus say about it?

> I give you a new commandment, that you love one another. Just as I have loved you, you also should love one another. By this everyone will know that you are my disciples, if you have love for one another. (John 13:34–35, NRSV)

> Do to others as you would have them do to you. . . . Be merciful, just as your Father [God] is merciful. (Luke 6:31, 36, NIV)

When arrested, Jesus could have allowed a battle to ensue. Instead, he did not fight and told his followers not to, either. In the midst of violence, he extended healing. When being crucified, he suffered physical pain and the abuse of the crowd, yet he asked God to forgive them. He even had the stamina to show compassion for the thief next to him. If any of us had been in such agony, would we have responded in this way? Jesus was clear in each case. This is why I cannot be a proponent of war. I want to do what Jesus did.

Life, however, often presents us with events that are complicated. While we commonly consider killing to be the worst crime someone can commit, I believe that what Hitler did was worse than killing. In addition to endorsing the deaths of several million human beings, he spewed poisonous propaganda, declaring that some people were inferior to others and therefore deserved to die. This included Jews, Gypsies, homosexuals, and anyone with a physical or mental disability, as well as those who protected these targeted victims or otherwise openly disagreed with the Nazi government. Innocent people were ripped from their families, tortured, and forced to witness the agony of others. Hitler's regime instilled fear around the world. Could we have justified standing idly by while he continued his reign of terror? Could we have stopped his influence without harming innocent bystanders while fighting him? Many of us writhe at the difficulty of such dilemmas. Yet we cannot stop here. If we follow Jesus, we must press on and look to him for better answers.

I must also admit that if someone I dearly loved was hurt or threatened in any way, I would certainly want to protect them. In such a case, it is possible that my base impulse could be to resort to physical violence to prevent or even avenge such an assault. I know that there are many others who share these feelings. Even so, I cannot find evidence in Jesus's ministry to support this kind of impulse. Jesus called us to rise to a higher plane, to trust in God. I have not perfected this. I only know that we should strive for it because he called us to do so.

⌗ The Uncommon Strength of the Amish

A recent example of what Jesus calls us to do can be seen in the response of the students, teachers, and families at an Amish school in Pennsylvania in 2006 after a gunman took them hostage, killed five girls, and wounded five others. Naturally, the entire community was devastated. But even as the heartbroken families were comforting each other in their terrible grief, they remained resolute about forgiving the gunman. Revenge would not restore their loved ones. They knew that forgiveness is the only way for anyone to heal. This community set an example for the rest of us. They rose to a higher level than we as a country have yet demonstrated. They remembered that Jesus told us to love our enemies and pray for those who mistreat us. They remembered his dialogue with Peter:

> Then Peter came up and said to him, "Lord, how often shall my brother sin against me, and I forgive him? As many as seven times?" Jesus said to him, "I do not say to you seven times, but seventy times seven." (Matthew 18:21–22, NRSV)

Surely the Amish community agonized over this. But they have set an example for us to show our children that retaliation is not a solution to a problem. Forgiveness is always a better way.

The Amish tragedy also reminds us not to jump to the conclusion that only people in other nations initiate violence. We must not forget Columbine and other school shootings, the Oklahoma City bombing, and various hate crimes, such as a young man in Wyoming being beaten to death for being gay, a black man in Texas being dragged by a truck to his death, or the scores of domestic beatings and murders that occur here every day. These are all acts of terrorism committed on American soil by Americans who grew up learning that violence is a way to display power. But Jesus gives us peace that is not as the world gives. (John 14:27) If we trust him, we must resist reacting reflexively with violence and instead respond with his peace.

Our Kids Get Hooked on Adrenaline

Consciously or not, we often carry within us the question that the disciples asked, "Lord, should we strike with our swords?" Our Amish brothers and sisters demonstrated the spiritual fortitude to obey the answer to this question as Jesus lived it. Yet we have created formidable stumbling blocks for ourselves as we attempt to do the same.

While many people can clearly distinguish among the concepts of *excitement*, *violence*, and *power*, others may have a more difficult time doing so. Many of us are drawn to action movies, including chase scenes, with the "good guys" making narrow escapes and "winning" in the end. From story to story, the definition of what constitutes a "good guy" enters a broad gray area, and violence may become equated with excitement and power.

A craving for power also influences what we find rewarding. Players of violent video games say that when they kill someone, they now "own them." Many of us crave more power in our lives, but children, especially, often feel small and may seek ways to exert some influence on their world. In addition, many kids say they are bored and are thus drawn to more and more "interesting" shows and games.

To further complicate the issue, violent images in advertising, television, movies, and video games are often intertwined with sexual images. Half-naked muscular men and scantily clad voluptuous women hold deadly weapons close to their bodies. "Hot" women pose in suggestive stances in the midst of multiple explosions. Viewers may then link violence with sexual arousal in their own minds.

Just as a drug addict will seek a stronger drug to achieve the same high they once attained with a milder drug, people can become addicted to adrenaline. As someone gets used to the intensity of injuries and deaths they see on the screen (and in the news), the images become less exciting. Anyone bored with the status quo will seek a more potent source of excitement. Children are more vulnerable than adults to this force. Often the faces of children watching violent images show little expression. What does this lack of expression mean? With the threat of continuing war in our real world, how concerned do we need to be that we could all lose our perspective toward violence? When students, elementary through high school, read about an act of aggression, I ask them how they think the victim felt. Many cannot articulate any feelings. Are they desensitized to pain? Are they deficient in verbal skills? Is it a lack of empathy?

Research shows an average hour of television viewing has four to five acts of violence. *Children's* programming, such as cartoons, average *twenty to twenty-five violent acts every hour*.[1] Young brains are much more impressionable than older brains, and we are exposing them to more violence, not less, than adults. By the time the typical American child reaches the age of eighteen, he or she has seen two hundred thousand dramatized acts of violence and forty thousand dramatized murders. According to Nielsen Media Research, during the 2006–2007 viewing year, children between the ages of two and eleven watched an average of three hours and thirty-six minutes of television per day. Children between the ages of twelve and seventeen watched an average of three hours and twenty-three minutes. The average U.S. household has their television on for an average of eight hours and fourteen minutes per day. This begs the question, are children within visual or audio range of shows that they are not necessarily documented as "watching," and are therefore witnessing even more violent acts than these statistics indicate?

---

1 The Lion & Lamb Project, Bethesda, Maryland, http://www.lionlamb.org/.

Study after study shows that children who watch more violence on television or play more video games commit more violent acts than those who are exposed to less media violence. Psychologist John P. Murray, PhD, states that when exposed to violence, children can become more aggressive, less sensitized, and more fearful about the world. Even though most children can tell us that they know television is not "real," Dr. Murray's MRI imaging research showed that children store memories of violent entertainment images in the same part of the brain where veterans store severe post-traumatic stress disorder memories.[2]

This phenomenon may be harder to fight than we think. The video game industry's net sales are estimated to be $40 billion per year.[3] To give us an idea of what this means, the book industry's net sales are $25 billion.[4] However, neighborhood games that children invent themselves, libraries, community centers, and museums are all relatively free sources of entertain-

---

2   John P. Murray, PhD, "TV Violence and Brainmapping in Children," *Psychiatric Times* 18, no 10 (October 1, 2001). Also available at http://www. psychiatrictimes.com/display/article/10168/54801. Dr. Murray is Professor of Developmental Psychology and the former Associate Vice Provost for Research and Director of the School of Family Studies and Human Services at Kansas State University.

3   PBS *Nightly Business Report*, November 29, 2007, http://www.pbs.org/nbr/ site/onair/transcripts/071129g/.

4   The Association of American Publishers (AAP), "Industry Statistics, 2007," http://www.publishers.org/main/IndustryStats/indStats_02.htm. This figure includes all types of books, including textbooks and audio books.

ment. No one benefits financially by manipulating kids to go to the library or take an art class, but there is substantial profit from selling violence.

Regardless of profit, violence in the media is having its effect on our children. I remember hearing about a road rage incident several years ago in which two men pulled over and got out of their cars for a face-to-face confrontation. One of the drivers, a teenager, proceeded to strike the other man in the head with a baseball bat. The man died. The teenager cried and told police that he was surprised that hitting the man in the head with a baseball bat would hurt him that much. While this particular person may have felt remorse for what happened, studies have shown that remorse is becoming less common.

In 1994, PBS aired a special by Bill Moyers entitled "What Can We Do about Violence?" [5] As part of his report, Moyers visited a number of juvenile detention centers and interviewed the inmates. In one facility for young women, he interviewed two young women who had tortured and murdered a young man who had given them a ride. They felt no remorse at all until they went through extensive therapy that focused on learning empathy—the experience of feeling someone else's feelings as if they were one's own. Through this program, they learned

---

5   According to PBS.org, this program was filmed in 1994 and, unfortunately, transcripts and videos of this program are not available.

to identify with their victim's feelings. They then felt remorse, and were able to offer sincere apologies to the family and friends of their victim. When Jesus says, "Do to others as you would have them do to you," (Matthew 7:12, NRSV) this is an appeal for empathy. He is asking us to see others as we see ourselves. If we did this, we would naturally show more compassion to others and would be more easily recognized as followers of Jesus.

Whose Actions Will Win Our Children's Attention?

If we reflect on what we see on television and in movies, we may notice that, more often than not, acts of violence are portrayed as the only possible way to save the day and are rarely punished. Titles of violent video games often imply that to play the game will make one noble and heroic. Our children, seeking recognition for themselves in a big, scary world, don't miss this fact.

As a teacher, I have heard many discussions among students in both formal and informal settings. I have taught students from first grade through high school. Almost all of the students I have met are insightful and have compassionate, noble ambitions. But many clearly express that when reacting to pain—whether on the playground, in family conflict, or in the world—their first impulse is often to consider violence as the best response. Some elementary students have proudly described to me what they know about the most advanced weaponry available to our nation. They name specific models of stealth planes and combat weapons. They describe features in detail, including how much damage each one can wreak. Whether or not these children are accurate in their weapon assessments is less important than their concept of the possible devastating outcomes and the way they pantomime militaristic actions, saying that they can't wait until they, too, can use these weapons and "blow people up" with them. While the children who verbalize these thoughts are in the minority, even these few are cause for alarm. And we don't know what the children who are listening silently to such opinions think of them.

When our children see us turn to violence as a first response to a tragedy, they learn to follow suit. In recent years, descriptions of violent events have become more graphic, even as the news reporters relating them speak in monotones.

A few of our children have even come to equate "offing people" with something that will win them adoring fans. Can this be anything but a serious abdication of our moral responsibility? I thank God for families like the one of the second-grade boy who explained his "What would Jesus do?" bracelet to me. His parents and his church are teaching him Jesus's version of what it means to be powerful. During the years I was in contact with this child, he was a conscientious student who showed kindness to others. Children like him provide us with signs of hope and strength for our future. Jesus's words here may sound weak by our society's standards, but they actually present us with a challenge greater than many of us have the courage to follow:

> Blessed are the merciful, for they will receive mercy. . . .
> Blessed are the peacemakers, for they will be called children of God. (Matthew 5:7, 9, NRSV)

> I desire mercy not sacrifice. (Matthew 9:13, NRSV)

Some of our children seek violence. Some wish to work for peace in their personal lives and in the world. Many have not yet decided what their role will be. Can we teach them to evaluate what they encounter and to choose wisely?

In the television show *Joan of Arcadia*, Joan, a high school girl, meets God in various guises, including a maintenance man, a cafeteria lady, a punk rocker, and a little girl. God talks with her and explains things to her, usually giving her a job to do that will provide the lesson she is meant to learn. In one episode, God tells Joan to do what she can to prevent her friend, Adam, from dropping out of school. Joan struggles as she seeks the right strategy. In the end, the only thing she can think of to do is to smash her friend's award-winning sculpture so that his door to the art world will be closed, at least until he has graduated. This demolition devastates Adam and causes pain to others who appreciated his unique work. Too late, Joan realizes the damage that she has done. She knows that destruction is not what God had instructed her to do. She cries and tells her mom, "I had a failure of imagination."[1]

We can all identify with this kind of failure at times in our lives. In this light, it is important for us to look around at what we are and are not doing for our children in various settings to encourage their imagination. Children can easily become proficient in video games. This often makes such games more attractive than open-ended, problem-solving ones. We don't provide enough opportunities for creative play that doesn't use electronic props, especially at home. In our school systems, because of the growing pressure for high test scores, more and more emphasis is placed on memorizing facts and using rigid formats to write papers and complete other assignments. Because many adults in our world today actually consider "play" a waste of time, less and less time and attention is allowed for free-flowing

---

1   *Joan of Arcadia*, created by Barbara Hall, aired 2003–2005 on CBS.

thought or creative problem solving. Our society is already paying the price for this in many areas of our lives, including choices that our nation is making in our interactions with the rest of the world.

President Dwight D. Eisenhower, an admired five-star general in the U.S. Army and famous for the important role he played in World War II, saw the need for imaginative problem solving. Identifying the problem, he said, "I hate war as only a soldier who has lived it can, only as one who has seen its brutality, its futility, its stupidity." [2] He expressed "a hope and a desire of the world that some way can be found to settle disputes around the conference table, not on the battlefield," and gave us all this challenge: "If men can develop weapons that are so terrifying as to make the thought of global war include almost a sentence for suicide, you would think that man's intelligence and his comprehension . . . would include also his ability to find a peaceful solution." [3]

Surely he is correct that we have the capability to find better solutions than what we have done so far. We must keep using our brains and our imagi-

---

2   Dwight D. Eisenhower, speech at Canada Club, Ottawa, Canada, January 10, 1946, http://www.eisenhowermemorial.org/speeches/19460110%20 Speech%20at%20Canada%20Club%20Ottawa%20Canada.htm.

3   Eisenhower news conference, November 14, 1956. John T. Woolley and Gerhard Peters, *The American Presidency Project* [online]. Santa Barbara, CA: University of California (hosted), Gerhard Peters (database). http://www.presidency.ucsb.edu/ws/?pid=10702.

nations to work toward the higher goal of peace.

What can we do to help? In February 2008, National Public Radio's *Morning Edition* featured two segments about children and play with research findings that apply to helping our kids at home and at school. Experts included neuroscientist Adele Diamond, psychologist Deborah Leong, cultural historian Howard Chudacoff, psychology professor Laura Berk, and others. These reports are well worth reading in full. Following is a brief synopsis.

When children learn to rely on themselves and each other for playtime (rather than on TV, video games, or highly structured games run by adults), they are likely to improvise props (rather than use commercialized ones) and make up their own games and stories. Doing this helps them to develop critical cognitive skills, including an important one called *executive function*. Essentially, executive function is the ability to regulate one's own behavior, which includes controlling emotions, resisting impulses, and exercising self-control, memory, and social flexibility. Even simple games in which children listen, think, and choose to act or not act, such as Simon Says, develop self-regulation. Building executive function improves attention span, increases reading skills, and promotes the kind of creativity and flexibility in thinking that helps us cope with life's unpredictability. "Poor executive function is associated with high dropout rates, drug use and crime," says the NPR report. In fact, it adds, "Good executive function is a better predictor of success in school than a child's IQ."

Make-believe play can make a child a better citizen, too. Psychology professor Laura Berk says, "One index that researchers, including myself, have used . . . is the extent to which a child, for example, cleans up independently after a free-choice period in preschool. We find that children who are most effective at complex make-believe play take on that responsibility with . . . greater willingness, and even will assist others in doing so without teacher prompting."

Just as healthy play contributes to strong executive function, so does setting it up, as the children decide what the game will be, who will play what roles, and what the scenario will be. And they often negotiate changes in the "script" as they go along— developing a talent that will be useful as they navigate through life. If we give our children plenty of opportunity to develop healthy executive function, then they will be more likely to contribute constructively to our society as they grow and mature. I have seen this in the classroom and in my personal life.

According to cultural historian Howard Chudacoff in the NPR report, another factor in child development is that before the 1950s, "play" was thought of in terms of *activities*. Since the 1950s, due to an increase in television advertising for toys, not just during the Christmas season but year round, play is thought of more in terms of *toys*.[4] The physical element of play is crucial, too. Marie Winn, author of *The Plug-In Drug: Television, Computers, and Family Life*, suggests that, in addition to the effect of violence on television, physical "play deprivation" may also be a cause of aggressive behavior.[5]

Personal choice and imagination can apply to something as simple as a child choosing a name for a stuffed animal. In recent years, toys have become more and more specific in their use, often with a character's name and a limited purpose emblazoned on the toy. Stuffed animals, dolls, and action figures now almost always come with a tag attached that states their name. Often children keep the corporation-given name, rather than choosing one of their own creation. This diminishes a child's thinking skills as well as their awareness that they can make choices, that they have some authority in their own lives, and that they are free to use their imaginations.

---

4   Some of the ideas in the above section were adapted from and inspired by data in Alix Spiegel's "Old-Fashioned Play Builds Serious Skills" (February 21, 2008) and "Creative Play Makes for Kids in Control" (February 28, 2008) in *Your Health* on NPR's *Morning Edition*, http://www.npr.org/templates/story/story. php?storyId=19212514.

5   Marie Winn, *The Plug-In Drug: Television, Computers, and Family Life* (New York: Penguin Books, 2002), 86–88.

Whose Actions Will Win Our Children's Attention?

When children are comfortable and well-practiced with using their imaginations, they can translate this skill to problem solving in the real world.

Of course, reading is another important activity for encouraging a child's imagination. It is no coincidence that children who read a lot will more often invent gadgets out of household items to use in their daily lives, for practical purposes or just for fun, than children who don't. I have observed this in family members, children of friends, and students. The children who invent the most are the ones who also carve out many hours of their free time to read.

Children have an innate craving to make sense of the world and their potential roles in it, and given the slightest opportunity, many love to put on plays for the adults in their lives. Such unstructured creativity is a marvelous way for them to develop executive function. I recently enjoyed the privilege of having a little girl sing to me. It was a spontaneous decision on her part. Before she began, she picked up a clear plastic cup and informed me, "This is my microphone." The inside of the cup fogged up as her song progressed, and I enjoyed her ad-libbed lyrics. What struck me most was her level of confidence. She didn't know me very well, but she looked me in the eyes and was calm and confident throughout our conversation and her performance.

When I walk past a certain house in my neighborhood, I often see elaborate multicolored chalk drawings on the sidewalk with pictures, arrows, directions, and tasks to perform before proceeding. While many mistakenly see these creations as trivial pastimes, I find them deeply encouraging. I see children who are confident about creating their own entertainment. More than that, I can envision children who know that they can have a hand in how their lives unfold. When they encounter challenges, perhaps they will not suffer a "failure of imagination."

Jesus demonstrates to us the power of executive function—the ability to be creative and flexible while regulating one's own behavior. He was constantly surrounded by pressure from others to become what his society and religious leaders wanted him to be. Their rules became more important to them than love for God or for one another. Yet Jesus remained steadfast to his ministry of love. Here is one example:

> Another time he went into the synagogue, and a man with a shriveled hand was there. Some of them were looking for a reason to accuse Jesus, so they watched him closely to see if he would heal him on the Sabbath. Jesus said to the man with the shriveled hand, "Stand up in front of everyone." Then Jesus

asked them, "Which is lawful on the Sabbath: to do good or to do evil, to save life or to kill?" [In Matthew 12:11, he says in the same circumstance, "If any of you has a sheep and it falls into a pit on the Sabbath, will you not take hold of it and lift it out?"] But they remained silent. He looked around at them in anger and, deeply distressed at their stubborn hearts, said to the man, "Stretch out your hand." He stretched it out, and his hand was completely restored. Then the Pharisees went out and began to plot with the Herodians how they might kill Jesus. (Mark 3:1–6, NIV)

Jesus knew the rules of his religious upbringing, and he chose compassion as a higher law. He was aware that his life was in danger, but he monitored himself, remembered what was important, and continued on the right path. We must follow his example and demonstrate compassion to our children, even when surrounded by pressure to do otherwise.

⧈ Which Action Hero Is Your Role Model?

Our experience of violence can come from TV, video games, global and local news, and sometimes firsthand experience of domestic violence, whether as a victim, a witness, or a perpetrator. While we don't have control over every event we encounter, we do have control over our exposure to media violence, the actions we take in our own lives, the words we say, and which leaders we choose.

I *love* America, but I will not be *proud* to be an American until we, as a nation, choose not to imitate those who attack us. Instead, I hope we will rise above our own thoughtless impulse to support violent behavior, and set a better example of how human beings, especially those of us who call ourselves Christians, need to behave. At this point in our history, it would be a fiction to say that America is a Christian country. When we live according to an "us versus them" mentality, we are not behaving like followers of Christ. Under our flag, we have policies that do not come close to resembling the example Jesus set for us.

Our children deserve to be shown more constructive ways to solve problems. It would benefit them to understand why we admire heroes such as Jesus, Gandhi, Mother Teresa, and Martin Luther King Jr., to name a few. Isn't it the people who choose nonviolent means to create peace that we most admire and revere? Why, then, do we persist in such impulsive, destructive behavior as killing unarmed civilians or torturing prisoners? When Nazis did this sort of thing, we were horrified. Why is it that many Americans seem to show so little conscience about our own nation's behavior? Where will it end?

In future elections, what will our children learn if they see us electing leaders who condone preemptory war and torture? The least of my concerns when voting is someone's political party. More important are the values of individual candidates. Any party can have members who lie, use illegal fundraising tactics, or are adulterous. We have reason to be skeptical about one-sided actions of anyone who serves only his or her own special interest group. We need a new breed of leaders who are willing to act with integrity and respect toward everyone. We need politicians who are truthful, insist on ensuring that every citizen's vote is honestly counted, work as a team with others, and show compassion toward all, not just their own group, whether political, ethnic, religious, or national.

As human beings in a big wide world, we can find tremendous comfort in staying connected with members of our tribe, those we identify by ties of descent from a common ancestor or with whom we form a community based on similar traditions or interests. Ancestry and tradition can certainly be positive, but sometimes people adhere to their group regardless of whether it is maintaining a positive moral path. In such a case, to continue loyalty without question reflects a lack of wisdom. Any group is dynamic and, unchecked, can become akin to a clique or a gang. Therefore, it is a healthy, conscientious, necessary response to confront the tribe if one feels that its principles have become skewed.

Many say we are a Christian society. A second-grade child who has been taught a central Christian message knows to ask, "What would Jesus do?" Do we want our children to grow up to be like people who initiate war — or like Jesus?

Facing Each Other Unarmed

Walking Jesus's path is not always easy. When caught in a warlike environment, the challenge to be compassionate and merciful can be daunting. For example, apartheid ruled South Africa from 1948 to 1990. Races were segregated, and the rights of non-whites were severely limited. If they objected, they were often subjected to torture, rape, kidnap, and gruesome deaths. As with the Nazis, it is hard to imagine how this ruling group—or any human beings—could even consider such acts. In 1990, apartheid was formally ended, and Nelson Mandela, an anti-apartheid activist, was released from prison, to become president in 1994. Finally some hope of peaceful equality began to flicker in South Africa. But change doesn't occur overnight. Racism and inequality remained, and a great deal of residual pain and suffering needed healing. In addition to the deaths that occurred during apartheid, many people had witnessed unthinkable atrocities against their loved ones. Who would not feel the pain and loss as if it were an open wound?

Then the Truth and Reconciliation Commission was formed, headed by Archbishop Desmond Tutu and supported by President Mandela. Hearings began in 1996. There were many goals. One was to fill in the details of what had happened during apartheid so that history would be complete and accurate. Another was to provide the victims with an opportunity to tell their stories, after decades of fear and hiding the truth. Progress is more likely to be made if the complete truth is disclosed. The perpetrators would come before their victims and the Commission, confessing in detail what they had done. Survivors could question them extensively.

So far, so good. But here is the part that not everyone could embrace: those who told the full story of their crimes could ask for amnesty.

From the beginning, there were mixed feelings about this process. Some felt that amnesty for people convicted of the abuses would create further divisions between whites and non-whites. That healing would never happen unless the perpetrators were punished. Others felt that truth telling, confession, and forgiveness would pave the way to lasting peace. The mixed feelings in South Africa continue, as does racial conflict. But some feel that the concept of reconciliation is in people's consciousness more than it would have been without the trials. It may be a long time before we have a clear picture of the full effects of the Truth and Reconciliation Commission endeavor. It is likely that most of the perpetrators would not have told the truth had amnesty not been promised. We don't know whether racial tensions would have become worse if no attempt at reconciliation had been made. Some believe that the process may turn out to have been a failure.[1]

But what would Jesus have done? What does he continue to call us to do? Even with its flaws, there seems to be a familiar reflection between the South African people's excruciating process and what happened to Jesus on the cross. Even though the Commission's role was not presented exclusively as a Christian response, it certainly appears to have followed Jesus's call to us to be courageous enough to both confess and forgive.

Could I have done what these brave South Africans did and faced my adversary in an attempt at reconciliation? I don't know. It is easy to speculate about this from my safe quiet little home. But it would be presumptuous of me to make a judgment about their response to such a complex crisis in a

---

1   Antjie Krog, *Country of My Skull: Guilt, Sorrow, and the Limits of Forgiveness in the New South Africa*, and introduction by Charlayne Hunter-Gault (1999), v–viii, (New York: Three Rivers Press, 2000).

world that is far from mine in physical, historical, and cultural realities. I must keep looking to Jesus for answers.

Further guidance might be provided by the example of the ten Boom family, who followed Jesus. Corrie and Betsie ten Boom, along with their elderly father, hid Jews and others who needed to elude the Nazis in their home in Holland during World War II. In a two-year period, it is estimated that they saved eight hundred lives. Finally caught in 1944, they were taken to the death camps, where Betsie and their father died. Their brother and nephew also died as a result of being part of the Dutch underground. Corrie survived to tell the story to the world. Following is a segment of her story that carries an important message for us today.

While suffering in the camps, Corrie and Betsie happen to find out the name of the person who betrayed them. As the days and weeks pass, Corrie becomes more inflamed with rage at the man who was responsible for their imprisonment and suffering. Betsie shows no animosity at all. One night, when Corrie cannot sleep, she asks furiously,

> "Betsie, don't you feel anything about Jan Vogel? Doesn't it bother you?"
>
> "Oh yes, Corrie! Terribly! I've felt for him ever since I knew—and pray for

him whenever his name comes into my mind. How dreadfully he must be suffering!"

Corrie picks up her narrative:

> Once again I had the feeling that this sister with whom I had spent all my life belonged somehow to another order of beings. Wasn't she telling me in her gentle way that I was as guilty as Jan Vogel? Didn't he and I stand together before an all-seeing God, convicted of the same sin of murder? For I had murdered him with my heart and with my tongue.[2]

Can we muster this sense of equality and compassion? Should we try? After betrayal, abuse, and deadly illness, these two women pushed through their suffering to follow Jesus's voice, which often speaks more quietly than anger does. Many who call themselves Christians choose to support a path of violence rather than to sincerely follow his example of peace. Tragically, the understanding of what it means to be Christian has changed so radically

---

2   Corrie ten Boom with John and Elizabeth Sherrill, *The Hiding Place* (New York: Bantam Books,1974),180.

that we are now faced with this question: Are we "Christians" or do we follow Jesus? Jesus's message was clear:

> You have heard it said, "Love your neighbor and hate your enemy." But I tell you: Love your enemies and pray for those who persecute you, that you may be children of your Father in heaven. He causes his sun to rise on the evil and the good, and sends rain on the righteous and the unrighteous. If you only love those who love you, what reward will you get? Surely the tax collectors do as much as that! And if you greet only your brothers, what is there extraordinary about that? Even the heathen do as much. There must be no limit to your goodness, as your heavenly Father's goodness knows no bounds. (Mathew 5:43–48, New English)

Anyone aware of the norms of our society knows that those who show love toward their enemies are most often rejected as wimps and fools. But do we follow Jesus, or don't we? Think about Jesus's life: his ministry, his acts, his words. The Gospels tell us that everything he did outraged the religious leaders of his time. He did not submit to the status quo. He

did not buy into their desire for a military messiah.
This disappointed many people who had considered
following him. But he held his ground. He preached
love.

How many people in the United States right
now think that war is justified? How many of us
call ourselves Christians? How many of us remember that Hitler called himself a Christian? We know
that merely saying we are Christian does not make
it so. Jesus reminds us to pay attention to actions
when trying to discern the truth about someone, including ourselves.

> Beware of false prophets, who come to
> you in sheep's clothing but inwardly are
> ravenous wolves. You will know them
> by their fruits. Are grapes gathered
> from thorns, or figs from thistles? In the
> same way, every good tree bears good
> fruit, but the bad tree bears bad fruit.
> (Matthew 7:15–17, NRSV)

Pain Is Universal

If the fighting in Iraq continues, the draft could be reinstated. If this happens, I could lose my nieces and nephew. There is nothing in this world that could ever prepare me for such a tragedy. It would break my heart and knock the wind out of me. I would never recover from the pain.

And, if I am an honest child of God, I am obligated to consider that if I would be devastated at losing a loved one, then every other person on this earth would feel the same under similar circumstances. I can imagine a woman in Iraq who savors life and loves her family. She works hard to make a living, just as I do. I can see a woman who loves sunrises, quiet mornings, fresh water, delicious food, and talking with friends. Perhaps she, too, has nieces and nephews, all of whom she adores. My heart knows how she would feel if anything happened to any one of them. When I picture her, I am brought to tears because she is like me. I understand her feelings because we were created in the same way, by the same God. Therefore, her heartbreak is my heartbreak.

Having spent my life contemplating Jesus's example of love and compassion, how could I not see it this way? Jesus didn't tell us to love just those from our own country. He certainly didn't die only for Americans. As much as our egos would like us to think otherwise, Jesus loves everyone else on the planet as much as he loves us. Jesus weeps when *anyone* is killed. We are not the sole proprietors of his compassion.

When we sense danger, do we draw our swords? Or do we follow Jesus? Are we ruled by our childish egos, or are we ruled by the best example God ever gave us? Until we see that *each* death in *every* country is of equal importance to the loss of those closest to us, we will never have peace in the world.

Some believe that peace will come once a war is over. However, in addition to the deaths on all sides and the people who mourn, even when a war is "over," countless veterans have been left so emotionally damaged by the trauma that they can no longer function in civilian life. Post-traumatic stress disorder (PTSD) can lead to drug use or violent crime.[1]

---

1   For one example, see Libby Lewis, "Court Aims to Help Vets with Legal Troubles," *The Impact of War*, National Public Radio, http://www.npr.org/templates/story/story.php?storyId=90016059.

Others find it difficult just to follow simple daily routines or function in relationships. Many of the homeless people we see are veterans. Our government has little interest in them. Indeed, most of our population has forgotten or avoids them, now that they have outlived their use. If you question this, start talking to the people who hold up cardboard signs on street corners; ask them if they are veterans. On many levels, war's effects are permanent. Perpetrators can become victims.

"All who draw the sword will die by the sword" can refer to a cycle of physical violence, but it can also refer to the psychological and spiritual damage shared by perpetrators and victims alike, as Betsie ten Boom so clearly perceived. She knew that the man who betrayed her family to the Nazis needed healing as much as his victims did. Jesus would also exhort us to pray for healing for suicide bombers and other terrorists. We can do this for our own troops who have caused harm. We can do this for all leaders who set the course for others.

▦ Gathering Our Nerve

What else can we do? How do we put our Christian beliefs into action? Walking this path is difficult, because we are often impatient and implementing peaceful solutions seems to take more time than war does.

Just a few days after September 11, 2001, I attended a women's conference at St. Catherine's College in St. Paul, Minnesota. At one of the meetings, I spoke with a woman in her late sixties who had lived in America for twenty-five years, but had lived her first forty-plus years in Saudi Arabia. She has since visited Saudi Arabia many times and has kept in touch with friends and relatives there. I remember her face and her voice as she gave her heartfelt opinion when I asked for her views of the current world situation.

She responded that many people from the terrorist groups in the Middle East are starving and have no education. When it comes to drastic measures such as terrorism, they feel they have nothing to lose. She pointed out that over many decades, America has supplied weapons and ammunition to *numerous* groups in the Middle East. What would really help, she said from deep in her heart, is for anyone who is capable to provide food and education, instead of guns. Only then would peoples' desires turn to more constructive pursuits.

Of course, such an effort could take many generations to prove itself. And we are an impatient culture. But what would Jesus advise? Part of Christian belief is in the miracles that Jesus performed. Do we really believe? Do we believe that he fed the multitudes with only a few loaves and fishes? Do we believe that God can do great things when we, with prayer and faith, feed others? Or is our faith so shaky that we will settle only for the most dramatic and immediate tactics?

President Dwight D. Eisenhower showed his awareness of the needs of the world in contrast to taking only a military approach. He said,

> Every gun that is made, every warship launched, every rocket fired, signifies in the final sense a theft from those who hunger and are not fed, those who are cold and are not clothed. This world in

arms is not spending money alone. It is spending the sweat of its laborers, the genius of its scientists, the hopes of its children. The cost of one modern heavy bomber is this: a modern brick school in more than 30 cities. It is two electric power plants, each serving a town of 60,000 population. It is two fine, fully equipped hospitals. It is some 50 miles of concrete highway. We pay for a single fighter plane with a half million bushels of wheat. We pay for a single destroyer with new homes that could have housed more than 8,000 people... This is not a way of life at all, in any true sense. Under the cloud of threatening war, it is humanity hanging from a cross of iron.[1]

A current demonstration of this awareness and the approach my Saudi Arabian friend suggested can be seen in the work of Greg Mortenson, which is described by *New York Times* columnist Nicholas D. Kristof. According to Kristof's July 13, 2008 column, Mortenson is an American man who

---

1   Angela Partington, Ed. *Oxford Dictionary of Quotations* 4th ed. (New York: Oxford University Press, 1992), p. 268. (Speech given in Washington, April 16, 1953).

builds schools in isolated parts of Pakistan and Afghanistan, working closely with Muslim clerics and even praying with them at times. . . . Now his aid group, the Central Asia Institute, has 74 schools in operation. His focus is educating girls. . . . To get a school, villagers must provide the land and the labor to assure a local "buy-in," and so far the Taliban have not bothered his schools. . . . he notes that the Taliban recruits the poor and illiterate, and he also argues that when women are educated they are more likely to restrain their sons. Five of his teachers are former Taliban, and he says it was their mothers who persuaded them to leave the Taliban; that is one reason he is passionate about educating girls. . . . Each Tomahawk missile that the United States fires in Afghanistan costs at least $500,000. That's enough for local aid groups to build more than 20 schools, and in the long run those schools probably do more to destroy the Taliban.[2]

---

2   Nicholas D. Kristof, "It Takes a School, Not Missiles," *New York Times*, (July 13, 2008), http://www.nytimes.com/2008/07/13/opinion/13kristof.html?ex=12166 12800&en=c5d9a9ad6353b482&ei=5070&emc=eta1. The book, *Three Cups of Tea*, (see Suggested Reading) describes Mortenson's work in detail.

More and more people are proposing practical alternatives to war. In *God's Politics: Why the Right Gets It Wrong and the Left Doesn't Get It,* author Jim Wallis, pastor, activist, and author, also speaks about putting our faith into action in practical ways. He states that "the world is desperate for a 'third way' between war and ineffectual responses — and it must be strong enough to be a serious alternative to war." In March 2003, before the war in Iraq began, Wallis and John Bryson Chane, Episcopal Bishop of Washington D.C., presented a six-point plan as an alternative to going to war. The plan actively addressed the crisis in Iraq caused by Saddam Hussein, and proposed to "recommit to a 'road map' to peace in the Middle East." The plan was known throughout our country and the world, including religious leaders, the White House, the U.N., and the U.S. State Department.

In addition, Wallis; Chane; Clifton Kirkpatrick, Stated Clerk of the Presbyterian Church, U.S.A.; Melvin Talbert, Ecumenical Officer of the United Methodist Council of Bishops; and Daniel Weiss, Immediate Past General Secretary of the American Baptist Churches in the U.S.A., met personally with Britain's Prime Minister Tony Blair to discuss the same points. They, and others like them, are well-informed and have the necessary abilities to propose many practical solutions. Even though the plan was not accepted by our leaders, it shows that there are workable alternatives available to us.

These approaches can be arduous. We may feel that our faith is being tested, especially because working in close proximity to those with whom we struggle can be frightening. Wallis points out, "To offer an alternative is always more challenging than just protest; it requires more work, creativity, and risk." [3] While this is true, Jesus was consistent in his message to us to put away our swords. He understood that much of our suffering comes from fear. This is why he repeatedly urged us to take courage. He reassures us that he is with us always. (Matthew 28:10) Surely this can strengthen our resolve to work harder for peace.

3   Jim Wallis, *God's Politics: Why the Right Gets It Wrong and the Left Doesn't Get It* (San Francisco: HarperOne, 2005), 43–55.

The Lure of a Glorious Battle

At times I think some Christians justify war because of Joshua's so-called glorious march on
Jericho. It was dramatic. We humans do like exciting climaxes to our stories. A catchy little Sunday
school song called "The Battle of Jericho" can be
jazzed up to attract more kids into youth groups.
Fortunately, we can move beyond this. Jesus
showed us a new way to live and relate to God. But
if you look at their choices, many Christians are
clearly stuck in the Jericho mentality.

Glorious battles are easy to visualize. Being on
the "winning side" appeals irresistibly to the ego.
We also love the story of David and Goliath, as if
the actual event were more important than its spiritual message. Our fears can tempt us to believe that
military might is wiser than having a close relation-
ship with God. In the Old Testament, the people of
Israel asked God for a king rather than a prophet to

lead them, because neighboring nations had kings and they felt a need to keep up with the Joneses. We continue our obsession with competition when we choose political solutions over spiritual ones. In addition, the human psyche is skillful at manipulating concepts, so we imagine that God wants *us* to win the battle — not *them* — as if there were not real human beings on the other side of the battlefield whom God also created and dearly loves. We forget that God loves us all and *yearns* for us to come closer to our Creator and each other.

While we often highlight the dramatic narratives in the Bible, we do not pay enough attention to the times of solitude that were so vital to the spiritual growth of Jacob, Moses, John the Baptist, and Jesus. It was at these times — not during battle — when they were able to hear God speaking.

A basic Christian belief is that God sent Jesus to earth to explain God in human terms. And what did Jesus really teach? He was big on themes of praying and listening, healing, loving, and forgiving. He never endorsed an exclusive tribal mentality. He challenged us all to turn our backs on warlike attitudes and rise to higher standards, telling us to "strive first for the kingdom of God." (Matthew 6:33, NRSV)

As Christians struggling in the face of conflict, we must ask: Are we stubbornly choosing to serve our egos? Or are we radical enough to believe that Jesus has a valid point? Do we believe what we preach in church—that Jesus is the Prince of Peace? Or do we dust off that maxim only at Christmas time?

The religious authorities in the New Testament were highly agitated about Jesus's behavior. Why were they angry? What did he do that was so offensive? He healed the sick. He healed on the Sabbath, which was even more shocking. He confronted the people who were financially exploiting religion. He cried when his friend died. He raised the dead. He fed hungry people. He refused to fight, even to defend himself. He urged people to make peace with each other. He forgave sins and urged us to forgive one another. He talked repeatedly about how deeply God loves us.

Is the outcome of Jesus's entire ministry to be that he is ignored or misrepresented? Do we follow him or not?

I believe that it is time for us as Christians to pray like we've never prayed before. The question of whether or not we are honestly living according to Jesus's teachings needs to be answered by God—not by a political party. Jesus's words and works were meant to draw us closer to God. If we are truly followers of Christ, then, like him, we will submit our hearts and our consciences only to our Creator.

In *God's Politics*, Wallis remarks that members of Congress "walk around town with their fingers held high in the air, having just licked them and put them up to see which way the wind is blowing. . . . The political leaders are really very good at figuring out the direction of the wind, and are quite used to quickly moving in that direction."

We might feel disillusioned about this, but Wallis continues, "You don't change a society by merely replacing one wet-fingered politician with another. You change a society by changing the wind." (Wallis, 21–22)

As Christians, we are called to love one another, not just locally, but globally, too. If we did this, the wind would surely change. We have passively blown with the wrong winds for too long. It's time to follow Jesus with our actions, not just our words. Wallis ends his book by quoting the late Lisa Sullivan, social activist, who said, "We are the ones we've been waiting for." (Wallis, 373–374)

I've been waiting for someone to help the mother in the big-box store. The natural first question, then, is: what would Jesus do? He would know what her life is like, what she needs. He would feel compassion for her and soothe her fears. He would engage her in conversation, as he did with the Samaritan woman at the well. (John 4:3–30) Jesus wouldn't force his values on anyone, but if she expressed interest, I believe that in some way, unique to her needs, he would teach the woman in the store about healing and empathy. Jesus could do these things for that mother and her child.

If we follow Jesus, the next essential question is: what can we do? It is easy to say that we can pray. But that alone does not get us off the hook. Jesus said, "Very truly, I tell you, the one who believes in me will also do the works that I do and, in fact, will do greater works than these." (John 14:12) For most of us, this may feel unnerving. But we can remind ourselves how often the One who loves us tells us to not be afraid. We can start with small steps and do what we are able to in the moment. We can remember people who have gone before us and have done great works. Jesus said, "I am with you always." (Matthew 28:10) Knowing that, how can we do anything else but step forward and love our neighbors, in our town or across the globe, as ourselves?

Suggested Reading

Grossman, Lt. Col. Dave, and Gloria DeGaetano. *Stop Teaching Our Kids to Kill: A Call to Action against TV, Movie & Video Game Violence.* New York: Crown Publishers, 1999.

Krog, Antjie. *Country of My Skull: Guilt, Sorrow, and the Limits of Forgiveness in the New South Africa,* introduction by Charlayne Hunter-Gault. New York: Three Rivers Press, 2000.

Maalouf, Amin, *In the Name of Identity: Violence and the Need to Belong*, English translation by Barbara Bray. New York: Arcade Publishing, 2001.

Mortenson, Greg, and David Oliver Relin. *Three Cups of Tea: One Man's Mission to Promote Peace . . . One School at a Time.* New York: Penguin Books, 2006.

ten Boom, Corrie, with John and Elizabeth Sherrill. *The Hiding Place*. New York: Bantam Books, 1974.

Tolstoy, Leo. *The Kingdom of God Is within You*. Translated by Constance Garnett. Mineola, NY: Dover Publications, 2006.

Wallis, Jim. *God's Politics: Why the Right Gets It Wrong and the Left Doesn't Get It*. San Francisco: HarperOne, 2005.

Winn, Marie. *The Plug-In Drug: Television, Computers, and Family Life*. New York: Penguin Books, 2002.

Acknowledgements

From the beginning of this project, Caroline Lehman has been my most enthusiastic supporter. She urged me on in her unique style when I needed it most. Thank you, Caroline, for your searching mind, challenging questions, thoughtful nature, and example of compassion.

Many thanks to Ann West for your spiritual integrity, your meticulous eye for nuances, and unrelenting persistence when working for clarity. I am grateful for all I learned from you.

To Lisa Meckel—gentle spirit, fellow introvert—thank you for listening, reading, rereading, asking thoughtful questions, and for encouraging me to keep moving forward. And while you may not see it, the way you teach children never fails to inspire me.

Thanks to Roy M. Carlisle for your objective eye, your perspective, for helping me to navigate the world of publishing, and for your friendship.

Many thanks to the reference librarians who helped me to locate the most reliable sources to double-check my facts. More and more, libraries are grossly underfunded, yet our librarians persist in bringing the world to us with great care, determination, and joy.

And, finally, thanks to my mom for setting the example that anyone can embark on new adventures. God always takes the journey with us. I'm grateful that I get to share this with you.

About the Author

Christie Monson is a writer, teacher, and educational consultant. She currently serves as a private tutor and consultant to parents and students. As a public school teacher, she taught gifted and talented, developmentally delayed, and learning disabled students. Monson earned a BA from California State University  Fresno and holds K–12 Multiple Subject, Learning Handicapped Specialist, and Resource Specialist credentials. She has served as an elder in the Presbyterian Church (PCUSA), and now meets with others who practice contemplative prayer.

Notes

The Jesus Question

Made in the USA